D0551105

EARTH BY NUMBERS

The Water Cycle

Nancy Dickmann

raintree

a Capstone company — publishers for children

Raintree is an imprint of Capstone Global Library Limited, a company incorporated in England and Wales having its registered office at 264 Banbury Road, Oxford, OX2 7DY – Registered company number: 6695582

www.raintree.co.uk
myorders@raintree.co.uk

Produced for Raintree by Calcium
Editors: Sarah Eason and Harriet McGregor
Designer: Paul Myerscough
Originated by Capstone Global Library Limited © 2018
Printed and bound in India

ISBN 978 1 4747 6534 3
22 21 20 19 18
10 9 8 7 6 5 4 3 2 1

British Library Cataloguing in Publication Data
A full catalogue record for this book is available from the British Library.

Acknowledgements
Picture credits: Cover: Shutterstock: Stephen Bonk (top), Petruk Viktor (bottom); Insides: Shutterstock: ArtMari 23b, BlurAZ 29t, Richard Bowden 4–5, Hector Conesa 28–29, Anton Foltin 8–9, Stefano Garau 15t, Dave Head 24–25, HurleySB 10, Jefunne 19r, Kazoka 12–13, Andrei Kuzmik 6–7, LiliGraphie 16, Alberto Loyo 25b, Nebojsa Markovic 18–19, Vladimir Melnikov 1, Nina B 23t, Dasha Petrenko 7b, Igor Rogozhnikov 14–15, StevanZZ 22–23, Stjepann 11, Swa182 21, TTstudio 12b, Merkushev Vasiliy 5b, Christian Vinces 26–27, Nickolay Vinokurov 27r, Trudy Wilkerson 20, Khongkit Wiriyachan 17, Pan Xunbin 9t.

Contents

Some words are shown in bold, **like this**. You can find out what they mean by looking in the glossary.

What is the water cycle?

All living things rely on water. About three-quarters of your own body is made of water! Our planet has vast oceans of water, but nearly all of it is salt water, meaning that we cannot drink it. Plants and animals rely on the **fresh water** that falls as rain and collects in rivers and lakes.

All the water on Earth – both fresh water and salt water – is constantly recycled in a process called the water cycle. When water is heated, it turns into a gas and rises into the air. There, it collects in clouds, then cools and turns back into liquid water. It falls back to Earth and eventually **evaporates** again.

EARTH BY NUMBERS

The amount of water on Earth has been about the same for millions of years. Earth's water is recycled again and again through the water cycle. In fact, the water you drink today may be the same water that a dinosaur drank more than 100 million years ago! Since then, it has probably evaporated and then fallen as **precipitation** millions of times.

The water cycle has four stages:

Precipitation:
Water falls from the sky as rain, snow, sleet or **hail**.

Condensation:
Water vapour collects in clouds. As it cools, it becomes liquid water again.

3

4

2

Collection:
The land, streams, rivers, oceans, lakes and other areas collect the water that falls.

1

Evaporation:
Heat from the sun causes water on Earth to evaporate and rise into the sky as **water vapour**.

This diagram shows the four stages of the water cycle.

Evaporation

A lot of water exists on Earth's surface. The oceans cover more than two-thirds of the planet, and even the large areas of land contain rivers, lakes and streams. The water in the oceans is salty, though the water on land is not. Any of Earth's water, either fresh or salt water, can evaporate as part of the water cycle. The water turns into water vapour and rises into the air.

Like all substances, water is made up of tiny particles called **molecules**. They are too small to see, even with a microscope! Every molecule is constantly moving, and the warmer each molecule becomes, the faster it moves. Molecules often bump into other molecules, which gives them more energy. Once a water molecule near the surface has enough energy, it escapes into the air. This is evaporation.

When water boils to make steam, it is changing from a liquid to a gas – evaporation in action!

EARTH BY NUMBERS

Like most other substances, water can exist as a solid, a liquid or a gas. The particles in a solid, such as ice, are tightly packed and cannot move very much. The particles in a liquid are less tightly packed, and they can move around more freely. The particles in a gas, such as water vapour, are loose and widely spaced. They move a lot, constantly bumping into each other.

Water does not always have to boil in order to evaporate. The water in a puddle evaporates on a sunny day.

Transpiration

Not all of the water vapour in the air comes from oceans and lakes. Some water vapour is produced by plants in a process called **transpiration**. Most plants send **roots** down into the ground. These roots suck up water from the soil, and tiny tubes inside the plant carry the water to all its parts, including the leaves.

The undersides of a plant's leaves are covered with tiny holes called **stomata**. These holes release water in the form of water vapour. The water vapour escapes into the air. Transpiration in plants is a bit like a person sweating, but when a plant is transpiring, its leaves do not feel wet. Plants transpire more in warm weather, when the sky is bright, or when it is windy. They transpire less when the air is humid. Around 10 per cent of the moisture found in air comes from transpiration. The remaining 90 per cent comes from evaporation.

Not all plants transpire at the same rate. Cacti do not transpire very much because they live in dry areas and need to keep hold of water.

EARTH BY NUMBERS

One reason that plants transpire is that it helps to cool them down, in the same way that sweating cools a human. Transpiration also helps plants take in more **nutrients**. When a plant loses water, its roots suck up more water from the soil. This water contains important nutrients.

The stomata in a plant's leaves allow water vapour to escape. They also allow the leaf to take in gases that the plant needs.

stomata

WATER—BY NUMBERS!

Earth has

1.4 trillion

cubic kilometres (332.5 billion cubic miles) of water. Water covers around 70 per cent of Earth's surface. Ice, **ice caps** and permanent snow make up 24 million cubic kilometres (5.7 million cubic miles) of water.

The United States use about

1.3 trillion

litres (355 billion gallons) of fresh water every day.

Water boils, or turns into a gas, at

100°

Celsius (212° Fahrenheit). But water can evaporate at much lower temperatures, even at room temperature.

In one year, a large oak tree can release

151,416

litres (40,000 gallons)
of water vapour through
transpiration.

Most of Earth's fresh water –
69 per cent – is frozen in **glaciers** and ice
caps. Just over 1 per cent is found as liquid
water at the surface, and about
21 per cent of this amount is found in lakes.
Rivers and lakes combined provide us with

92,950

cubic kilometres (22,300 cubic miles)
of fresh water.

30

per cent of
all fresh water comes from beneath
the ground. The water soaks into the
ground deep below Earth's surface
and resurfaces at springs.

11

Condensation

Water vapour in the air does not always stay as a gas. The higher you go, the cooler the air becomes. Cold air cools down the rising water vapour. When it gets cold enough, it turns back into a liquid. This is called **condensation**. It is the reverse of evaporation.

You can see condensation when you breathe warm air onto a window. Tiny water droplets form on the glass and make it look cloudy. The water vapour in your breath is cooled as it comes into contact with the cold glass, and it condenses into tiny droplets.

When water vapour in the air condenses, it can take several different forms. The dew you see on grass in the morning is a type of condensation. It is caused when water vapour comes into contact with cold ground. Fog and mist are also types of condensation.

Fog and mist often form at night, when the temperature falls. They disappear in the warmth of the day.

When you pour a cold drink, tiny water droplets soon form on the outside of the glass. Water vapour in the air condenses when it hits the cold glass.

EARTH BY NUMBERS

Warm air is lighter than cool air. This is because its molecules are more spaced out. When the ground is heated by sunshine, it warms up. This causes the air just above it to become warmer, too. The warmed air rises because it is lighter than the air around it.

13

Clouds

Even on a clear day, the air is still full of water vapour – you just can't see it. But when water condenses high in the sky, it forms clouds. Clouds are masses of water droplets in the air. The water droplets are so small and light that they are able to stay in the air, instead of falling to Earth.

We've seen that cool air can cause condensation. Condensation can also happen when a mass of air becomes **saturated**. This means that it contains so much water vapour that it cannot hold any more. The molecules of water vapour are pressed closer together, and eventually form droplets.

Water vapour condenses more easily when it has something to stick to. It can condense on tiny particles of dust, pollen or other substances in the air. When tiny water droplets bump into each other, they stick together, and eventually form a cloud.

EARTH BY NUMBERS

There are many different types of clouds. Cirrus clouds are thin, wispy clouds found high in the sky. Stratus clouds are low, flat clouds. Cumulus clouds are low-lying clouds with a thick, puffy shape.

Cumulonimbus clouds (sometimes called thunderclouds) are heavy and dense. They can cause heavy rain, hailstorms or tornadoes.

High, wispy cirrus clouds are bright white during the day, but they can also take on the colours of the sunset.

CONDENSATION—BY NUMBERS!

An average-sized cloud can weigh about

400,000

kilograms (875,000 pounds), which is as much as a fully-loaded 747 aeroplane! A really big cumulonimbus cloud can be 10,000 times heavier. Because this weight is spread out over a huge area, the cloud can stay airborne.

The water droplets in a cloud can be far smaller than the full stop at the end of this sentence, at just

0.01 millimetres

(0.0004 inches) long. The largest droplets are about 5 millimetres (0.2 inches) across.

The bottom of a cumulus cloud may be only 365 metres (1,200 feet) above the ground, while a cirrus cloud floats at about

12,190

metres (40,000 feet) above the ground.

The highest a passenger jet normally flies is about

11,900

metres (39,000 feet).
At this altitude, it will be above nearly all the clouds in the sky.

The water droplets in a cloud are so tiny that nearly

3 million

of them fit into every 28 litres (1 cubic foot) of air.

A towering cumulonimbus cloud can reach more than

19

kilometres (12 miles) up into the sky, and it can weigh up to 1 million tonnes.

Precipitation

Precipitation is any form of water falling from the sky, and it is probably the easiest part of the water cycle to see in action. The most common type of precipitation is rain, but there are also many other types, including sleet, snow, hail and drizzle. Some types of precipitation, such as rain, are liquid water. Other types, such as hail, are solid ice.

Many clouds never release any precipitation. Warm air rising from the ground helps to push a cloud up and keep it in the air. The droplets of water in the cloud are often too small and light to overcome these **updrafts** and fall to the ground.

Sometimes, however, the droplets grow big and heavy enough to fall from the cloud as rain. This often happens when they bump into each other and clump together. Snow forms in a similar way: water droplets freeze into tiny **ice crystals**, and stick together to form snowflakes.

EARTH BY NUMBERS

A lot of the water in clouds comes from water that has evaporated from the salty oceans. So why isn't rain salty?

The answer is that when water from the oceans evaporates, the salt is left behind. Only pure water forms clouds.

When the temperature is cold, precipitation can fall as sleet, snow or freezing rain.

When ice crystals clump together to form snowflakes, they often form beautiful patterns.

FALLING WATER—BY NUMBERS!

It can take more than

1 million

water droplets to make a
single raindrop.

Mount Waialeale in Hawaii
holds the record for the highest
average yearly rainfall:

11 metres

(37.5 feet) per year. But the
rainiest year ever recorded was
in Cherrapunji, India, in 1861,
when 23 metres (75.4 feet) of
rain fell!

The ice crystals that form
snow take up more space than liquid
water. Depending on the temperature
during the snowstorm,

33 centimetres

(13 inches) of snow on the ground
contains the same amount of
water as 2.5 cm (1 inch) of rain.

Most hailstones
are less than

2.5

centimetres (1 inch)
across, but the largest
can be up to 15 cm
(6 inches) in diameter!

If all the precipitation that fell
on the United States mainland stayed
on the surface, it would cover the entire
area to a depth of

76

centimetres
(30 inches).

During a heavy rainstorm, the
average raindrop will be about

0.25

centimetres (0.1 inches) across, and will
fall at a speed of 7 metres
(22 feet) per second. If you marked out
an area of 0.1 square metres
(1 sq foot), approximately 46 drops will
fall on it each second.

Collection

When precipitation falls to the ground, it has to go somewhere. This stage of the water cycle is often known as **collection**, and it can take many forms. For example, a lot of rain falls directly on the oceans, where it can eventually evaporate again.

When rain falls on the land, a small amount lands in rivers, streams or lakes, but most of it soaks into the ground. It may eventually enter a stream, or it may go deeper into the ground. Some of this underground water returns to the surface, when an **aquifer** empties into a lake or river.

When snow falls in cold climates, it is often stored on the surface. In some places, enough snow builds up to form glaciers and ice caps. Some of this frozen water will eventually melt and flow into rivers.

When rain falls, a lot of it seeps deep underground, where it is collected in an aquifer.

EARTH BY NUMBERS

An aquifer is a layer of rock deep underground that can store water. The type of rock in an aquifer has small openings that liquids and gases can pass through.

When water seeps into the ground, it often ends up in an aquifer, where it can be stored. People drill wells to reach the water in aquifers.

Glaciers flow very slowly down to the sea, where enormous chunks of ice often break off to form icebergs.

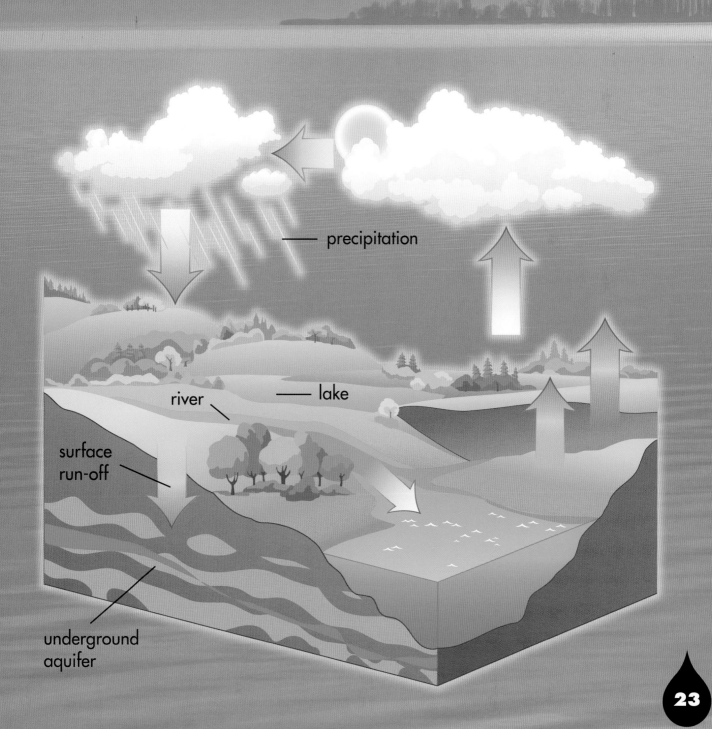

precipitation

river — lake

surface run-off

underground aquifer

Surface run-off

Some water that falls on land flows back to the oceans in a process called surface run-off. It happens when rain falls on land that cannot soak up water. This may be because the rocks are too hard to soak up water, or because the ground already holds as much water as it can.

Flowing water always moves downhill. After a heavy rainstorm, you may see water near the kerb flowing down the road. The same thing happens in the wilderness, where surface water moves from higher ground to lower ground. As the water trickles down, it collects in small channels that join together to make larger ones. These channels have many different names: creeks, brooks, streams or rivulets, for example. As the water moves downhill, the streams eventually join a larger river and flow down to the ocean or sea.

Many rivers enter the ocean at an estuary, where fresh water and salt water mix. Estuaries are important habitats for wildlife.

A lot of the salt in the oceans actually comes from rocks on land. As water flows over land, it breaks down rocks. These rocks contain many different chemicals, including salts. Some of these chemicals are carried by streams and rivers all the way to the oceans.

Run-off can also occur when snow melts. For example, the snowcap at the top of a mountain may melt in the spring, and this water feeds fast-flowing mountain streams.

COLLECTION—BY NUMBERS!

Around **1/3** of the precipitation that falls on land returns to rivers and oceans. The other two-thirds either soak into the ground or evaporate back into the air.

The largest aquifer ever discovered is in Australia. It covers **1.7 million** square kilometres (661, 000 square miles), which is around 22 per cent of the entire country. Scientists estimate that it contains 65,000 cubic kilometres (15,600 cubic miles) of groundwater.

Some water has a very long journey back to the sea. From the source of the River Nile, water must travel **6,650** kilometres (4,132 miles) to reach the Mediterranean Sea.

Of all Earth's rivers, the mighty Amazon releases the most water. Every second it releases more than

169,900

cubic metres (6 million cubic feet) into the Atlantic Ocean! The Amazon is the source of approximately 20 per cent of all the fresh water released by rivers into the oceans.

On average, around

3.5

per cent of the oceans is made up of salt. Some lakes and seas are much saltier, though. The Dead Sea, in the Middle East, is one of Earth's saltiest bodies of water. It is made up of about 34 per cent salt.

We need the water cycle

When water flows down a river and returns to the ocean, it can evaporate, and start the cycle again. Some water may stay trapped in a glacier or underground aquifer for a long time – perhaps thousands of years. Other water may be used for drinking or to water crops before evaporating or transpiring again. The water cycle is a complicated process!

If we didn't have the water cycle, life on Earth would be extremely difficult. We depend on precipitation for the water that makes plants grow. If there was no rain, farmers could still get water from **wells** to water their crops – at least until the aquifers dried up – but huge areas of forest would die unless they were watered. Rivers and lakes would eventually dry out, either by evaporating or emptying into the oceans. Without doubt, we need the water cycle!

EARTH BY NUMBERS

Humans can affect the water cycle in a number of ways. For example, we build **dams** that trap water in rivers, stopping the water flowing back to the ocean. We use wells to take water from underground aquifers. We even spray chemicals into clouds that help make rain fall. Some of these actions can harm the environment.

A rainstorm can spoil your day, but rain is incredibly important. Without it, life on Earth could not exist!

We can't live without fresh water, so it is important not to waste this natural resource.

29

Glossary

aquifer layer of rock, sand or gravel underground that contains water

collection stage in the water cycle where precipitation is collected after it falls, either on the surface or underground

condensation process of changing from a gas to a liquid

dams structures, such as walls, built across rivers or streams to keep them from flowing

evaporates turns from a liquid into a gas

fresh water water that is not salty

glaciers large masses of ice that move very slowly down slopes or across land

hail small, round pieces of ice that fall from the sky

ice caps large, thick sheets of ice that spread out over the land

ice crystals shapes formed when water freezes in regular shapes

molecules smallest units of a substance that have all the properties of that substance

nutrients substances that help humans, animals and plants to live and grow

precipitation water that falls from the sky as rain, snow, sleet or hail

roots parts of a plant that suck up water and nutrients from the soil

saturated not able to hold any more water

stomata tiny holes on the underside of a plant's leaf that allow water and gases to move in and out

transpiration process by which a plant releases water vapour from its leaves into the air

updrafts currents of air that are moving upwards

water vapour water in the form of a gas

wells deep holes dug in the ground to reach water or other resources

Find out more

Books

Liquid Planet: Exploring Water on Earth with Science Projects (Discover Earth Science), Tammy Enz (Raintree, 2016)

Solids, Liquids and Gases (Essential Physical Science), Louise and Richard Spilsbury (Raintree, 2014)

The Science Behind the Wonders of Water: Exploding Lakes, Ice Circles and Brinicles, Suzanne Garbe (Raintree, 2017)

Weather (Eyewitness), DK (DK Children, 2016)

Websites

Discover more about the water cycle at:
www.bbc.co.uk/guides/z3wpp39

Learn more about protecting our water supply at:
www.bbc.co.uk/education/clips/zg7xwxs

Find out more about the water cycle at:
www.dkfindout.com/uk/earth/water-cycle

Index